# DRUNKEN ROBINS

## By David Oates

BRICK ROAD

POETRY PRESS

Grateful acknowledgement is made to the editors of the
following publications in which some of these poems first
appeared: *Albatross, Asahi Evening News, The Athens Observer, black
bear, bottle rocket, Brussels sprout, chiyo's corner, cicada, haijinx* (online),
*hummingbird, japanophile, Magic Stream Journal* (online), *mayfly, point
Judith light, Reflections* (online), *shiki haiku salon* (online),
*spin/kokako, Woodnotes, Word of Mouth* (online)


Cover photograph: © Adam Edwards | Dreamstime.com
Author photograph: UGA Photographic Services
Cover design by Keith Badowski
Brick Road logo by Dwight New


Library of Congress Control Number: 2011922995
ISBN-13: 978-0-9841005-1-4
ISBN-10: 0-9841005-1-2


Published by Brick Road Poetry Press
P. O. Box 751
Columbus, GA 31902-0751
www.brickroadpoetrypress.com
ALL RIGHTS RESERVED
Printed in the United States of America

# DRUNKEN ROBINS

*For Jane, John and Caroline*

# Author's Note

This is a collection of favorites from over twenty years' accumulation of haiku and senryu, mostly written while living in rural Appalachia for 6 years and then Athens, Georgia for 16. I have tried to follow the precept of catching the crucial details of a moment that struck me, giving those to you without my specific reaction.

I try to make each poem as brief as it reasonably can be, while following the usual practice among the majority of serious haiku practitioners of not focusing on 17 syllables in 3 lines. In following the advice of Basho, I have not tried to write as if I were in medieval Japan, but rather have drawn inspiration from the nature and human nature I see around me.

This collection would not exist if my friend Keith Badowski had not been kind enough to tell me that he liked my haiku and senryu. Thank you Keith, and thank you to Ron Self of Brick Road Poetry Press.

I've had fun making these. I hope you enjoy them, too.


David Oates

Grand Ole Opry
from the dark, camera flashes
lightning bugs



after communion
he finds a bit of meat
between his teeth

April, 3 AM,
up with the baby again
first birdsong




holding tiny frog in her hands
look on six-year-old's face

mountain drive—
winding and dipping,
climbing and braking, then
oh, God, a sign
"Hill"


little boy's command
hundreds of plastic soldiers—
only a few stand

purple clematis
around the mailbox
mailman eyes bumblebees


vacant lot—
in the grass,
small pecans

such break dancers!
even the pickpocket
stops to watch


bare kudzu vines swallow the tree
from under them, pale spring leaves

waiting for job interview
he buffs his shoes
on the back of his pants


the runoff
pauses—
icicles

winter street
tires rip slush


an hour and a half
before gallery opening
the artist agonizes
over shoes

summer day,
reading with my six-year-old
faint smell of chlorine




my friend who was a butcher
on his hands, old white lines

new dogwood flowers,
small, green, like unripe fruit
delicately upcurved


ballet teacher coaching from the wings,
along with her sharp whispers
her own feet cross, point, cross

sycamore in winter sun
a pretty fat girl
lifts her arms




off the freeway
among gas and burger joints
bird's call

Sunday dinner at the Nu-Wray Inn
antique music box announces meal
then tinkle of iced-tea spoons



mom at home, two kids
enjoys long chat with telemarketer—
time for a vacation

end of the school day
on the parking lot asphalt
many squashed acorns




circus—
the elephant's toenails
painted white

morning after, driving 65
one aspirin escapes his hand


winter sun—
an old dog sleeps
by the swing set

she's in good spirits
till two weeks after first chemo—
too much hair in the comb


chemotherapy
she practices drawing on
eyebrows

mountain farmer tends
the burning field's margin
scorched boot smell



engineering classroom
different colored chalk rectangles
on the light brown ceiling

he teaches Logic and Ethics
never picked for jury




rushing by the scenic overlook—again

older brother, as Easter bunny,
steers the youngest towards eggs
as the middle fills her basket

little boy sleeps with a smile
bulldozer dream

the sight of home's hills
after a week at the beach
first swallow of wine


rusty old car
decorated today—
"JUST MARRIED"

gray dawn,
motion-detecting porch light
flicks on
as a catbird hops


after miscarriage
against the wall
a new crib

Times Square
mud puddle
flashing



the poet conjures angels
in a rolling voice—
his dog loudly, steadily,
licks herself

digging in
his pocket for change
pacifier



in the long grass
by the bird feeder
a cat seems to doze

Southern *Nutcracker*
backstage, whispered again and again
"'Scuse me."


bought used house
on bedroom wall
glow-in-the-dark stars

the bonsai
on my desk
small fall


computer running on couch
as she naps, toes on keyboard
180 pages of z's

in the street gutter
small stream of clear water
surface etched with x's


fit of giggling
in the *corps de ballet*
not one step missed

bobbing two inches
above middle of the road
dingy pink balloon


the land is dark
the sky shines bright
in a cow pond

eats sushi
while driving at night
mushy lump—wasabi!


Danish elementary school,
on the front lawn,
statue of a nude woman

in the shadowed hollow
fugitive snow




busy waitress
talking to herself,
"I'm going to have a good day!"

awake for a moment
in the middle of a winter's night
blanket's sparks




keeps watering
dead bonsai

as the naked dancer undulates
on her chest, gold cross flops


she walks in the meadow
a quail flies up
two hearts race

he looks up and down the block
then erases the meter maid's
chalk mark



autumn rain
after picking it off my car
the dogwood leaf's texture

in back of pet store
long discussion: is this mouse
too big for boa?




after the near miss
away from my car for a week
grass sticking from the wheel covers

freeze, then warm spell
makes the hackberries ferment—
flock of drunken robins

wife snores
"shhhh," he says,
"shhhh."

gray day walking to work
past the church playground—
the slide is wet


how beautiful our hillside farm
now that we're moving

rainy day, after the ice storm,
all the pale flashes
of the tree breaks




autumn
wanting to have a child
new blood

Labor Day weekend
last swim in the outdoor pool
with each lap, more leaves




middle-aged doctor
finds osteoarthritis
in her own hands

spring, Tennessee mountains
nailed to the side of the barn
five yellowed raccoon skins


backstage
the sound of ballet slippers
sweeping wooden floor

bruises on the waitress's hips
sharp-cornered tables




landing at LaGuardia
between runways
dandelions

wife and daughter in the car ahead
punctuating unheard conversation
hands

hungry baby
sucking on leather chair

so quick the eyes can't focus
an owl through headlights' wash


with dad at computer
eight-year-old says, yet again,
"It's *my* Christmas gift!"

mountains near Mt. Airy,
church advertises "Live Nativity Scene—
Drive Thru"



Amsterdam—hanging from the fence
a heavy bicycle lock
sawed through

at the mall stand
for airbrushing t-shirts, license plates
the young employee
wears a beret


afternoon of a gray day
pink morning glories
still fresh

morning
toddler puts glasses on nose
of sleeping father


old oak
snow accents
dark branches

son and granddaughter
sing "Happy Birthday" on phone
like him, tone deaf




bare dogwood
hung with pine needles
Christmas is near

fat actor
before his big scene
tightens belt




rummaging in the mass of vines
extracting a perfect cluster
of green tomatoes

minister reads verse,
congregation fights laughter—
cardinal attacking window


outdoor concert
after everyone's gone
calls of tree frogs

nap at the stoplight
the car behind
for alarm clock


blank computer screen
reflects bare sycamore branches
against a blue sky

after a sip of beer,
young girl listens to the band
then lights her lollipop stick



by the power line
amputrees

November 1st,
cutting off daughter's bedroom light
star-tipped wand flashes




soon after the big dog died
using the can opener,
outside, no whine

from a pickup's window
graceful bare feet
with dirty soles


chatting
with the pretty pharmacist
by the condom rack

suburban sidewalk
chipmunk scurries, man smiles
cat darts


you know the old man's dead or down
his fields erupt with cedars

the knife slips—
string of red beads




thirty-four-year-old woman
in for cancer-caused hysterectomy
the cheerful nurses
wear smocks with pastel dinosaurs

ballerina with veil
about to go on stage
"I can't see, I can't see!"

spring schoolyard
a long golden hair tumbles shining
in the air

church play
the part of Jesus
preacher's kid




two inches of snow
nine-year-old Georgia girl
won't come inside

Knoxville classic-rock station—
every singer's throat
is white




walking late at night
ripe dogwood blooms lit
by the porch light

toe-shoes solo
clop clop
cloppity clop


young possums the dogs killed
almost as ugly as adults
little curled paws

he unplugs computer sound
so his family won't hear
train whistle




male bulldog
missing one hind leg
sniffs a tree

ninety-year-old man
watches cherry blossoms


spring morning,
in the scuffed place under the swing
fire-ant mound

meeting for the first time
lunch with someone else's wife
studying the menu




putting away glass
on the shelf by another
chime

on the topic
"My Most Important Day"
fourth-grade beauty writes
about getting saved
at Pizza Hut




in the road,
by steep driveway
crushed red plums

daughter, seven,
reading the Bible, asks,
"Daddy, what's circumcision?"

tossing the bouquet—
young career women
keep hands at their sides

something walking
down my ear
milkweed seed

vacant oddity shop
by winding mountain road
"Coming Soon—Jesus"

friend tells me
she's pierced her nipple—
didn't need to know


warm sunny January day
kicking a green Skittle
on the sidewalk

what is that
rubbery, cool, in coat pocket?
forgotten daffodil


Valentine's Day
someone shivers while sleeping
on a park bench

mows lawn in makeup
and bright, flowing evening gown
the recluse's daughter


on the neck of
the worn teddy bear,
flea

lady with Alzheimer's says of her son
"This is my brother Jim,
who died recently."


honeymoon
until she's written thank-yous
the bride can't relax

downtown, working late—
through window, the sound
of beer bottles shattering




north Georgia, March
the top of the pine stump yellow—
pine pollen

icicles from car grill—
sixteen-year-old's sparse beard


sits down to write
after long time away—
white page

near the barn-swallow roost
a moth camouflaged
as a bird dropping




three years later
he still has wedding-cake
on his jacket

dogwood branch in a vase
on the second day
blossoms' elegant droop


frenetic ballet
when the music's low
the dancers' gasps

just shaved off his beard—
how long till he stops
shampooing his face?

 

late April,
driving up the mountains
redbuds—again!

during pregnancy,
sips no-alcohol beer, then sighs,
each day for a month




bare trees, pale—
mountain fog

why are we called *homo sapiens*,
"Man the wise"?
we picked the name




red maple seeds
on pavement
melted crayon

rural liquor store
in the corner, among the beer cases
a four-year-old watches *Sesame Street*

ice storm
the sound of a pine branch
snapping, falling

daydreaming at stoplight
Baroque French horn on radio—
the car behind harmonizes




on the bumper of the crushed car
riding stacked on the trailer bed
"God Is A Good God"

sunny fall day,
the graveyard maples lay down
a thick, colorful quilt

wrote their own vows
mother asks,
"Did they mention God?"

Athens, Georgia,
outside pawnshop he opens trunk
gets his bass drum


sunset in the rearview mirror
see the sky ahead reflected
on my glasses

dog so eager
to sniff another's spray
wet nose




getting late at the strip club
dancer stalks off—
"Hey! It don't cost you to clap!"

on the Stop sign
the loser's campaign stickers


from nearby hillside
watching football practice
teenaged dwarf

parked bike in Amsterdam
broken off morning-glory vines
through the frame



the little dogs charge
across the pine floor—
toenails!

while my two-year-old son is away,
I see a fire truck with the ladder raised


at the red light
three waiting drivers, all dance
in their seats

in the library book,
dried and pressed flat,
someone's tomato sauce


just switched
from stick shift to automatic
awkward feet

away from family a month
pacing him in motel parking lot
a white plastic bag rolls




dog pisses
on a traveler's tire—
Internet

June pawnshop
well-worn wedding rings



he came to reunion
in rented Cadillac
no one remembered him

on the pale asphalt
in front of Revco,
little red left mitten


climbing into bed
a bit of the blanket
warm from her body

on the sidewalk at the red light—
joggers accumulate
shifting from foot to foot


dark drizzly day,
petals from the Bartlett-pear trees
spin and flutter down

reads a poem about a dead friend
raises her voice—
cappuccino machine




(interstate billboard near Greensboro NC)

"Harper's 2—
Gentleman's Club
And Exotic Car Wash"

cool, sunny fall day
car dodges yet another
acorn-fat squirrel




midnight—
trying not
to call her

Wendy's lunch with the
exercise-class ladies
lipstick on white straws




lives for a year near el tracks
wakes at 2:00 one morning
when train doesn't pass

interstate driving
streak of firefly glow
on the windshield


walking arthritic dog,
each step on pavement
one set of toenails drags

on the ancient battlefield
torn red Coke cup


holding my sleeping son
shoulder blade on my hand
breath on my shoulder

spin cycle
the trailer vibrates




daffodils up,
willows green
first whiff of skunk

after twenty years
I fly in dreams again—
not as high




smoothing toothpaste in
apartment nail holes before
the landlord's inspection

Georgia in February
fingering seed packets
in the refrigerator door



months after moving back
from separation
one load of possessions
still in his car

walking with his wife
little male poodle
on a leash


months after the blizzard,
field cedars still lean

messy office—
steps on ketchup packet
pop!




his four-year-old daughter watches
as he rubs Rogaine on his skull—
"It's not working, Dad."

ruffling, sunlit, gleaming
as if illuminated from within,
the dead skunk's white fur




hand-lettered sign below toll-plaza window
"Yes, This Is 70 West
Denver Is 540 Miles"

as he shaves,
crack and flash of lightning, nearby—
by itself, electric toothbrush starts




wet winter morning
the sun strikes black branches
their tops shine silver

finishes her candy bar—
even on her back,
chocolate




small town South
an "Ah men" congregation
with an "A men" preacher

fall woods
the only green leaves
on a broken maple branch


after Christmas
bright and full
recycling bins

autumn twilight
last purple martin?
first bat

over the bar
at the Danish brew pub
a net full of shoes*

*when someone bought a large beer in an
expensive glass, the bartender made the
customer leave one shoe

this ladybug goes
round and round, then round again
on the rim of the cup—
who am I to laugh?

captured quail who escaped
in suburban woods
its call unanswered

long business trip
alone in room with TV
a blanket over the tube




outside the minimarket
small stray dog, skittering back and forth,
reads the emotional weather

hot day in Memphis
people pushing a stalled van
with a temporary tag




they hung a pirate flag
from their front porch
within a week, stolen

leaves all fallen
the trees' graceful silhouettes
at twilight




motel carpet
darker place in the shape
of an iron

at party during drought
guest wonders
should I flush?




mountain trail
four-year-old on dad's shoulders
sharing blackberries

ballet recital
pink feathers float
from dancers molting




across the hot pavement
bird shadows

music box stops
the mind still plays
the tune

# About the Author

David Oates teaches math and English and hosts *Wordland*, a public-radio show on WUGA, Athens, devoted to poetry, fiction, and comedy. His own writing has been published in little magazines and newspapers. His previous haiku and senryu collection is *Shifting with My Sandwich Hand*. Sow's Ear Press published his short-story and poetry collection *Night of the Potato*. He has worked as a reporter, and wrote for the comic strip *Shoe* in the 80's.

Please visit our Brick Road Poetry Press web site
for more poetry collections
that entertain, amuse, and edify:
www.brickroadpoetrypress.com

**BRICK ROAD**

**POETRY PRESS**

In the following bonus pages, samples are provided
from Barry Marks' collection *Possible Crocodiles*,
published by Brick Road Poetry Press
and winner of the Alabama Poetry Society's
Book of the Year (2010).

From *Possible Crocodiles* by Barry Marks

## Teaching the Angels to Dance

The wings, that's the worst problem.
Their wings scrape the carpet and trip
cherubim and seraphim alike until,

with a snort that somehow
hangs musical in the air,
they shoot to the ceiling for a breather.

"Listen to the beat," I plead, but
drum and bass seem to pass through them.
They are lost in melody.
Michael closes his eyes and
unconsciously takes off;
he bumps his head on the chandelier,
settles back to the floor,
blushing, shrugs an apology.

Raphael stumbles into the china cabinet,
Tzaphkiel and Tzadkiel collide,
Metatron practically somersaults over the sofa,
and none of them able to translate their innate grace,
their light-drenched, aerodynamic beauty,
into the simplest of steps.
I joke that perhaps I should find them a pin,
but that falls flat before empty, beatific smiles.

Only Death seems to get it right,
the perfect partner, following my lead,
her dark eyes glowing,
her balance flawless as
she twirls and spins so light on her feet,
she makes me feel like Fred Astaire -

until Gabriel cuts in
with a whisper that this is one dance
I should probably sit out.

From *Possible Crocodiles* by Barry Marks

# There Is Nothing Oppressive
# As a Good Man

There is nothing oppressive as a good man
      who has already thought of everything you are feeling
      who is there for you at the end of the line
      who politely prolongs by thinking about something
else and wants you to hold still goddamnit so he can fix you.
      Who denies himself everything you need.

There is nothing oppressive as a good woman
      who cares and cares and cares
      who wants to be everything you should want
      who knows that she is always right and is perfectly
willing to admit that you are, too.
      Who denies herself everything you need.

They do not want to be a bother, to intrude on
      the body in which you are embedded.
They do not want to take anything you have
      until you cannot take it anymore.
They lie awake next to you, petrified with fear
      of lesser men and women, then rise
      to the insistent morning light,
      clutching your future and floating away,
      calling your name quietly so as not to wake you.

From *Possible Crocodiles* by Barry Marks

## The Lion Sleeps (Better) Tonight

Lion got into therapy because he had
issues, mostly aggression control
but also feelings of inadequacy since
the day he learned that tigers were
larger.  He's doing ok, but I'm afraid
shark's marriage went aground
despite years of counseling.
His wife complains that he's still
a cold fish.

Giraffe won't speak,
rhino refuses to wear her glasses
and strikes out blindly at everyone,
zebra can't work, and boa still
approaches every hunt as a potential
crushing defeat, but

elephant is doing fine in the twelve-step
program he started the morning after
he gambled away one of his tusks,
and I am pleased to report that mandrill
has been sober for seven months.

Every day he recites the serenity prayer,
goes to his meetings
("Hello, I'm Mandrill. . . ."),
stays away from fermented bananas

and has even stopped worrying
about the size and color of his behind.

So I guess there's hope for us all.

From *Possible Crocodiles* by Barry Marks

## Song

this is not a song
it is a poem about a song
or about something about
a song

you know the one, it goes
*da da da dum da de da*
that one
or another one maybe

it doesn't matter really
you choose the song
close your eyes
clear your thoughts
and let the song start

that one
now you will hear it
the rest of the day
I hope it's one you like
and not one your six year-old
sings over and over
or the theme song
for your wife's religion

I hope it is your song
your best song
a song so true to you

you could have written it yourself

that song is the one I mean
the one I write about
the one that tells you
there is more to you
than blood and snot
more than money and words
more than the four corners of your body
there is something that can last
there is a God
and He can carry a tune

From *Possible Crocodiles* by Barry Marks

## I Stop to Ponder the Stentorian Colors of the Day

The railing down from the deck
to the garbage cans was wobbly, and
since you left, I've certainly had
time on my hands,
so I unretired my rusty box saw,
found an old two-by-four
and some three penny nails
and got to work.

A dog was barking, yelling his name
at the dog next door,
*Big Dog Who Swims! Big Dog Who Swims!*
To which his neighbor barked back,
*Dog Who Hates Cats!* and
some nearby mutt yapped,
*Mama's Favorite! Mama's Favorite!*

A cardinal was shouting,
*Beauty!* A mockingbird said
the same, of course.

A chameleon shot out of the hedge,
stopped by my foot and, turning from green
to almost-brown, sneered,
*You can't see me,* then skittered off.

The sky was whispering until
I looked up, and it screamed,
*Forever!*
to which the grass responded,
*Joy is fragile!*


And the saw
sang in my hands
and the wood?
Come on, now. An old two-by-four
with a bent nail in its heart?
Everyone knows dead wood
has nothing to say.

Made in the USA
Lexington, KY
30 May 2011